7 Yummy Lessons

ABOUT LIVING A FULL LIFE

KerryAnne Henry

7 Yummy Lessons: About Living a Full Life

www.Girlletmetellyou.org

Available in these formats:

ISBN - 978-1-73671598-7 (Paperback)

ISBN - 978-1-73671590-1 (eBook)

Library of Congress Control Number: 2021905735

Names: Henry, KerryAnne, author.
Title: 7 yummy lessons : about living a full life / KerryAnne Henry.
Other Titles: Seven yummy lessons
Description: Union, NJ : Greenhouse Press, [2021] | Includes index, a bonus section of recommendations for restaurants (both locally and internationally) as well as a bonus section of questions for self-paced exploration related to the topic discussed in each chapter.
Identifiers: ISBN 9781736715987 (paperback) | ISBN 9781736715901 (ebook)
Subjects: LCSH: Self-realization--Anecdotes. | Self-consciousness (Awareness)--Anecdotes. | Mindfulness (Psychology)--Anecdotes. | Food--Psychological aspects--Anecdotes. | Quality of life--Anecdotes. | LCGFT: Anecdotes.
Classification: LCC BF637.S4 H46 2021 (print) | LCC BF637.S4 (ebook) | DDC 158.1--dc23

Published by Greenhouse Press | Union, NJ

For volume and wholesale/resale pricing, please contact 7yummylessons@gmail.com.

For Mom and Justin.

"Eating is so intimate. (It's very sensual.) When you invite someone to sit at your table...you're inviting a person into your life." – *Maya Angelou*

TABLE OF CONTENTS

Something Light To Get Us Started.. 8

Chapter One
More Than A Sweet Treat !
(How To Live A Marshmallow Life) 11

Chapter Two
Who's Coming To Dinner ?
(The Company Makes The Meal).. 15

Chapter Three
Commit To The Meal
(Stick-With-It-Ness) 20

Chapter Four
Finally, The Secret To Great Oxtail
(Savor The Flavor) 24

Chapter Five
Meal Prepping
(Mind Over Matter)... 28

Chapter Six
Simmer Down The Gravy
(Soul Food) 32

Chapter Seven
Spit It Out!
(It's Ok To Say No).. 35

Chapter Eight
*Brawta*Yes, You Should Try It! 38

Deeper Levels Of Yummy... 43

Bu-Nu-Nu-Nus... 48

Acknowledgements... 52

About The Author 57

Something Light To Get Us Started.

About two decades ago, I discovered writing, more accurately discovered writing as an outlet. Short poems at first, often filled with frustrating attempts of me trying my hardest to process life, relationships, school, friendships and childhood. As you may imagine, over time, the work transformed. It shifted to longer discussions over time. All the while I focused on how I was experiencing the world and how I was making sense of what was happening in and around me. I would always say to my sister MJ, "girl I need to write a book because the things happening to us can't possibly just be happening to us." I imagine that's how many people feel, the need to validate their experience in the world so as not to feel alone. Those early conversations with friends were the first time I spoke out loud about my desire to write a book. It started as an idea to share what I then called "Black Girl Chronicles" or some iteration of this name. Over the years, it's transformed into the body of work you see here. Battered by fear, drenched in "what-ifs," and dragged across years that questioned its worthiness to arrive in this yummy space.

Over time this body of work helped me process some things, share out loud and hold some things up to the light, bear witness to the ways I was growing and the limbs I sometimes had to prune in the process. At its crux, its most simple purpose is to ensure that I don't forget. In many ways, it's an exercise in overcoming fear in very small ways and enjoying some of the most delicious foods along the way.

Before we dive in, I'll also note here that this culmination of work reflects development over time. Rooted in these lessons are reflections of countless conversations with girlfriends, boyfriends, friends and incredible people I've connected with on this journey. In many ways, this work is as much theirs as it is mine; we co-created these experiences. And while my formulations and resolve are my own, they wouldn't exist in the absence of rich connections.

Speaking of my formulations, I'll confess that since this body of work spans over a decade, there are times when I question the methods through which I learned certain things. I've grown a great deal since having experienced some of the stories accounted for here. But, like many people, I'm constantly reminded that even when I've learned a lesson, it's not inherently "locked in." I have to practice it - daily. So, I encourage you to keep this in mind as you share this space.

In case you're asking why 7 Lessons - the number 7 signifies completion.

The intention for this body of work is two-fold. The first being this: writing and reading sustain my peace. I think that's true for many people; my aim is to be and share peace where I can. The second being: to serve as permission (if needed!) for anyone seeking to live more freely and to do the thing you've been afraid to do. If you're reading this, I hope you take it as proof that action cures fear. Stop waiting for perfection. Your creativity and creations are critically valuable. Even more so because without you taking action, it cannot otherwise find its way into the world. And if you find some use in sharing this space with me, if something in these pages connects with you, maybe inspires you to live more boldly, then I'm grateful to be part of your story.

CHAPTER ONE

More Than A Sweet Treat !

(How to live a Marshmallow Life)

I was an eager new social worker in my early 20s when I first learned about the Marshmallow challenge. I was excited about changing the world, clutching my notebook and pen intensely with big dreams about the change I could make. On this specific day, I was excited to prove my worth in the new worker training session. The type of training where everyone's wearing their white rectangular name tag, nervous about saying the wrong things yet slightly excited about what's ahead. Early in the training day, the instructor introduced the Marshmallow challenge; she told the rules, gave us our materials, answered a few questions and then yelled, go! I, like my team members, immediately got to thinking and doing of winning this thing. Truth be told I'm not even sure what the prize was; most likely, it was purely bragging rights until the next competition. We were off to the races. Some leaned over the table, others kneeled on chairs, some standing to get the best vantage point. We started by sketching our thoughts on paper. Someone asked, how on earth will we balance a marshmallow on noodles? We were all wondering the same thing. As you can imagine, the trials ensued. The leaders in the group naturally took charge. When their ideas didn't quite work after a few attempts, we tried someone else's. And so it went on, for about 10 minutes - maybe less. Yes, this is a timed challenge...because what's a competition without a buzzer to beat.

If you've ever been involved in any corporate teaming event, then you've probably tried the marshmallow challenge. If you haven't, you're in for a treat. I won't get into all the details of the challenge - as you can review them for yourself[1]. The gist of the challenge is that teams are given minimal items (spaghetti, string, tape, and a marshmallow) with the competition being whichever team builds the tallest structure using only the materials given - wins! O, and the marshmallow has to be on top. That's the catch!

Years later as I recount this, I don't recall whether our team won; although my ego would like to think so. But I'll never forget the lessons I learned from that afternoon's team-building session. It's applicable to life, love, living and everything in between. It taught me how to Live a marshmallow life.

It turns out the most successful group of people in this challenge are kindergartners, beating engineers. Likely because their minds are free and fearless, not bogged down by what's possible and what's failed so many times before. They also accept failure quickly and use what they learned to improve their next try. They're failing fast and often and

1 The Marshmallow Challenge originated with Dennis Boyle (IDEO) and was later presented at TED (c) by Peter Skillman and Tom Wujec. https://www.ted.com/talks/tom_wujec_build_a_tower_build_a_team

using what they learned to inform the next attempt. WOW! It seems like a simple concept, but for damn sure as adults, we often completely miss this process.

The truth is, as we get older life teaches us certain lessons, one of which is - it's helpful to stick to the course. But life is also about balance and finding that sweet spot. It's always a dance and not linear. The quicker we accept the lesson from failure, the more quickly we can use the lesson to do better next time.

In the infancy stages of my real estate investment journey I was gung ho about investing in single-family homes. I read most of the newbie books like John Schaub's "Building Wealth One House at a Time,"[2] practically lived on the Bigger Pockets website and podcast and did the research. Nobody could tell me ANY-THING. For months I banged my head against the wall wondering why my plan wasn't working. Despite talking to many experts, going to Meet-ups and watching hours of content on YouTube University, I wasn't finding deals. I wasn't having a good go at this strategy. Then I had an aha! moment....you know the one when you're in the car driving home from work overthinking life and things just become uber clear. The clarity was this - The strategy isn't best for my current conditions. I needed to track and adjust. By conditions I mean, investing in single family homes can be an awesome investment under the right circumstances but certain things must align...the amount of money you have to invest, the demographics of the neighborhood, long term investment goals and market conditions (for example, is it a buyers market?) I had to find my sweet spot, the strategy that would work for me. First, I needed to accept that at this point, single-family homes weren't in my lane. So I re-focused on multi families, and within 4 months I had a deal under contract. It was so important not to get bogged

---

2 Schaub, J. (2016). *Building wealth one house at a time*. New York: Mc-Graw-Hill Education

down by ego. Sometimes we spend so much time working at something that we fear how we'll look to others if we change course.

What I've learned for certain is it's best to fail fast and often. Be fearless. Easier said than done - YES! Once you do it the first time and feel the liberation, trust me the second time will be easier. In failure you will have learned what did not work and use it to your benefit the next go round. Change is the only constant in life, THE ONLY **insert clapping hands**! It's by living a marshmallow life that you become comfortable with change; you make it a practice, you accept the lesson learned faster and use that lesson to build a better plan. Either that or keep getting beaten in life by kindergartners.

CHAPTER TWO

Who's Coming To Dinner ?

(The company makes the meal)

The company makes the meal. In fact, my most memorable meals have been ones shared in great company. They bring fun, great conversation, laughs, all necessary ingredients for a fulfilling life and meal. It's the same with life; surround yourself with people who are fun, progressive, positive and not necessarily "like-minded," but share your core values. Oprah once said, "you don't want people to just ride in the limo with you; you need people who will push the limo if it breaks down."

In recent years I started taking trips solo as a means to replenish myself. However, I must confess that on every single trip I've met someone new and we've shared a meal. And while I was content reconnecting with tranquility solo, a shared meal with a new friend was also part of the rejuvenation process. I'm always open to these shared experiences. People are surprisingly kind, ready to share and eager to connect.

One of my favorite memories was meeting Ade. We met in the "lobby" of a small inn on Nwigwe beach in Zanzibar. I use the lobby loosely, as this was more of bed and breakfast than a hotel. Initially, I was hesitant to talk with him. As a woman travelling solo, I don't practice being very friendly with most strangers. But in such a small space, while I waited for the staff to arrange transportation for the next day's excursion- it felt rude to not speak. Besides, his vibe seemed mellow. After a few minutes of talking, I learned he was Zanzibarian, a marine biologist and headed to the beach for some relaxation. He asked about my trip so far then shared practical travel advice and suggestions for local eats. A refreshing and unexpected discussion. A few nights after our initial meeting we met at a local restaurant in Stone Town. The restaurant sat on the edge of the beach, just a few feet away from the bustle of the Forodhani night market. The sea much like a nearby companion was gently lapping the sea wall- soft, calm and unassuming. We talked for a few hours and though I don't recall what we ate (though I'm sure it involved fish because on an island, there's really nothing better than seafood), I remember the meal was good. The conversation was better. I learned about his work on a global scale and more exceptionally, his work with local fisheries and fishermen and women - teaching them deep-sea survival skills. We connected about the perceptions of the West regarding certain religions and his lived experience that in no way mirrored the stereotypical beliefs generally promoted about his religious group. We're still connected, dare I say friends. We occasionally commiserate about politics, work, the world, writing and balancing all we must, to thrive.

When you think about the details of planning a dinner party, the intention needed to support every meticulous detail; the parallels are uncanny. From the seating arrangements, to the dinner courses, the decor, the mood, the music, the ice breakers and guided discussions. The same meticulous nature is required when curating our lives. Being intentional about whom we extend an invite into our lives, with whom we share our energy, those with whom we not only enjoy dessert but cleaning up the post-dinner mess. If you've ever hosted a dinner party, you understand the final product - all the laughter, joy, glee-filled chatter- is the result of tremendous planning and not just hoping things work out alright. The same rules apply to the company we invite and nurture in our space. Healthy relationships and interactions don't just happen; they result from intentional planning, intentional work and expression of emotions, intentional boundaries and a shared commitment to the relationship.

The immediate thought that comes to mind when I consider my dinner party guests is summer 2019. It's a humid 100 degrees out in NYC. Five friends and I are lugging dinner wear and actual dinner, across Manhattan. Yes, half-dozen people, dressed in all white, lugging folded tables and chairs, igloos, baskets (containing dinner and dessert) through the hot (and smelly) NYC subway. It's the type of day where the already interesting scents of the city are emboldened by the heat and made more aggressive by peak commuter crowds. It smells like hot stink- if that's even a thing. We eventually leave the subway and emerge onto crowded city streets. Every other minute feels like a new apology to a passerby for bumping into them and/or their belongings. They are going about the regular work day. This is in fact a work day, it's Tuesday afternoon. But here we are, heading to a secret location somewhere in the city, to connect with a couple of hundred other adventure-seekers for an impromptu dinner in the park. More aptly, Dinner en Blanc. When you see pictures of this event online, they're elegant, often picturesque. What's missing is the actual journey to the dinner table. On this particular day, we were on the journey- sweating from every crevice possible. The side-bar lesson here is: do this event when you're young enough to not care about the hustle or old enough to know better (AKA you can afford help and catering). Anyway, within minutes of arriving at the location (Rockefeller Park) the skies looked bleak. We made our tables with formal dinnerware, opened some wine, and finalized the dinner spread - we felt fancy! We were there maybe 30 minutes when the skies opened up—torrential rain. Initially, we thought it would be a summer shower..a few minutes and it'll pass. It poured non-stop for 30 mins, then came the wind, lightning and thunder. At this point, the organizers officially shut down the event. My friends and I were cuddling in pairs under the umbrellas we brought - initially hoping we wouldn't actually need them. Welp. We started packing up, throwing out soaking wet bread, folding wet tables and chairs. And yes, it's still a downpour - as if someone spilled a bucket of never-ending water. All packed up; we joined the streams of soggy dinner guests leaving the park. The rain is relentless. It's now whipping sideways. As if to aggressively usher us out of the space. Somewhere between packing up and exiting the park, we put the umbrellas away. They were in fact, useless at this point; we were already fully drenched - and it was still raining. Throughout the ordeal, I remember hearing one thing consistently - laughter. Sure we were initially annoyed. After all, we were looking forward to a nice dinner, in a nice space on a nice summer night. Instead, we got some "unexpected magic." A chance to see each other's true character. We laughed so hard that night; I'm sure I shed tears. If you were a stranger watching us - you'd probably think something was wrong. We were having too good a time for a rained-out event. We laughed at the irony of being soaking wet for what was intended to be a chic night in the City. We laughed at how aggressive the rain was as if it had a vendetta. We laughed at every damn thing that night. Not because we were delirious, but I surmise because we chose to see the hilarity, the good in our shared experience. We chose to enjoy each other's presence and use the current circumstance as an opportunity to share pure joy. I've never had that much fun while soaking wet and hungry. These are the people you need at your dinner party; the ones who find the silver lining; they help you lug the "stuff" and create a space for shared joy.

The 2020 pandemic has really driven home the practice of intention when it comes to the company we keep. More than before, I found myself being incredibly intentional about the people I connected with (both physically and emotionally). This being my first pandemic and all - I've learned a few lessons. One of which is, when life's uncertainty is apparent, there are select people you chose to spend time with - even when you have all the time in the world. Those people are positive, hopeful, deep and critical thinkers, intentional about their own life and growth, they aren't afraid to love and live vulnerably, they are patient. These are the people in my Top Five - lol! Jokes aside, if I were to go through my phone log and take inventory of the people I've connected with most during a time of forced isolation - they reflect the best parts of myself. They are people who inspire me everyday in a myriad of ways.

CHAPTER THREE

Commit To The Meal

(Stick-With-It-Ness)

*F*ull disclosure, I was an avid procrastinator. Like last... lasssst minute. While in Grad school, true to form, I procrastinated on doing process recordings. Now, any social worker reading this knows the BANE of any social work education experience can be process recordings ESPECIALLY when you have limited material to actually process. If your field placement is live and hectic- and you have a lot of interaction - then by all means, there is no lack of material to process. Which means just sitting down to write it up. I digress. Bottom line- I procrastinated. To the point where I had to meet with the Dean of my program about whether or not I could continue as a student. Holy sh**! Talk about being scared. In my mind, all I could think about was how procrastination got me here. Needless to say, I had a decision to make, accept that my BS had gotten me here and maybe this Masters of Social Work (MSW) program wasn't for me OR accept and face my BS then move forward in spite of it. I considered my wins along the way. I was a good student; I valued the degree and what it could mean later on in my work and career. So, I chose the latter. I decided to get an MSW when I applied 2 years previously, and I decided only death would stop me from following through with that goal. It wasn't an easy choice, especially since there were no financial incentives connected to getting an advanced degree. There was no immediate compensation for this advanced degree; it wouldn't necessarily open promotional doors immediately. So, the decision had to come from me purely wanting to finish what I started and seeing the value in doing so.

Mistakes are part of the journey- this is something we must accept early in any and every process. Expect them. Plan for them. Plan for what can go awry because so much can and often will.

Along this same vein, my mom used to always say learn to make at least one good meal; your signature meal. Perfect it. Make it your "go to" meal, whether for yourself or your loved ones. For me, this is brown stew chicken and mashed potatoes. I say that with pride and a huge smile on my face because if you know me well - you understand that I love to eat way more than I like to cook. I think that's true for most of us. Cooking isn't my strong suit (more about this later). What's important to note here is, you don't perfect your signature meal the first time. You must stick with it. Make it often. Play around with it, substitute ingredients, heck - make it even when you don't have all the ingredients you need. Make the dish for others, particularly someone who will be honest with you so you can get their feedback. This allows for the opportunity to honestly assess your skills.

No truer example of this was present than on a trip to Ghana when I served as a teaching assistant. I had the pleasure of working with an amazing group of super-smart, enthusiastic, beautiful (both inside and out) young women. Ladies who I'm certain, now almost 10 years later, are about the business of changing the world. On this trip, I met Kendell* who in all honesty, I made certain assumptions about at our first meeting. She was gorgeous; I'm talking Iman-model gorgeous. She dressed the part and was meticulous about how she carried herself. During the 6-week stay in Accra, we cooked many meals at home and lacked many American ingredients. This girl was the queen of substitutes and her dishes (though not elaborate) were delicious! I could tell she was not a novice at cooking, and more importantly, she wasn't afraid to try new things to make it work. She was not punkin' out of a meal if we didn't have all the ingredients it called for. Because of this, in some ways, she became the go-to person when we were cooking - or at least she was my go-to person! Watching her navigate the kitchen made me think how confident she was in her abilities and being committed to making any meal possible.

Committing to the meal is about making a decision and seeing it through. It's about staying the course. It's a lesson we can readily apply in so many areas, namely when approaching how we'll achieve our goals (both long-term and short-term). When comparing the two, long-term goals by design often require more time and subsequently, we must set a series of smaller goals in between. This, among other things, creates the opportunity for small wins and keeps us committed for the long run.

Stick-with-it-ness is imperative to growth. But it's not an overnight lesson. Learning its importance is only achieved with time and practice. Committing to and practicing your signature meal, whether filet mignon or tuna melts, teaches the significance of consistency. And this is a lesson that can also be applied to every single area of life, be it dating, work, fun, relationships, life goals...sh** even in Candy Crush.

Consistency is the result of commitment. It's crucial, but me telling you that doesn't automatically make it important. When you assess the areas of your life where you've had success, I'm certain you will find consistency. What you do occasionally means very little compared to what you do every day. It's why habits are so crucial. Both when kicking bad ones to the curb and nurturing the good ones.

So there you have it, stick-with-it-ness/commitment → consistency → habits → goal achievement. If you're like me, it's helpful to link concepts together especially, when moving from abstract to practical minutiae.

CHAPTER FOUR

Finally, The Secret To Great Oxtail

(Savor The Flavor)

*L*ife happens fast; time is always moving more quickly than you think. Living in the technology age means what's hot in the AM is old news by lunch...sheeeit more accurately 5 minutes later. Information seems to move at the speed of light. But life can only be enjoyed by being in the moment, not living in the past and not existing in the future.

Take time to feel the texture on your tongue, let the flavor seep into your taste buds and find residence there at least momentarily. Allow yourself to be engulfed in the scents of the meal. Indulge in the mouth-watering taste of it all.

A few years ago (circa 2014) while looking for ways to create a more intentionally peaceful life, I came across Headspace[3] (I think through a podcast). Anywho, it was a god-send. I never thought meditation was my thing, but being connected to a higher power and being tranquil has always been right up my alley. Headspace makes this easy. I try to use it as I start every day. It heightens my awareness of a peaceful space, so as I move throughout the day and feel myself being dragged along by whatever the predominant movement is (work, play etc.) I'm always acutely aware of how to get back to the moment, get back to the center, get back home.

Along this same vein, it's helpful to make a practice of creating opportunities for tranquil spaces to exist in your life in various ways. For example - I've found there's no more perfectly tranquil moment than being in nature and just listening. Whether on a hike or listening to birds on a quiet Sunday morning. In these moments it feels as though everything falls away and it's just you sitting in the arms of that moment. Nothing else matters. Not the bills, not work, not the to-do list, not the person I need to call back; nothing else matters. It's a beautiful space to exist. It's an honest space, one in which we get to fully just be. Moments like these remind us of our connection to the universe, our connection to a higher being, something greater than ourselves.

I've also found these beautiful moments with food. My favorite dish is brown-stewed oxtail, home-cooked by my mother. In my early 20s I penned a poem dedicated to the experience of enjoying this succulent meal. I lost it for a few years but later found it. And I'm delighted every time I read it! It chronicles a perfect Sunday afternoon dinner, where the scent of oxtail wafts in the living room from the kitchen and in that moment - all is right with the world. When the savory brown stewed beef connects with the taste buds on your tongue, it's a match made in heaven. Now, heaven-sent ox-

---

3 Headspace does not pay me to advertise. More information can be found via their website.

tails don't just happen. What most people may not realize is the secret to great oxtail starts with selection and trimming of the fat. Nothing is more disappointing than delicious oxtail gravy hitting your tongue only to be followed by a glob of fat. Your tastebuds need connection with that slow-stewed meat. I don't make the rules; they just are. It tastes like home, nothing shy of perfection.

I've had similar experiences at local restaurants - particularly in NYC. One in particular, Gramercy Tavern, stands out for an exceptional meal. My friends and I celebrated a birthday there years ago and we still talk about the meal to this day. The experience was exquisite. Not because it was pricey, since I've had ok food that was very pricey, it was exquisite because the flavors were intricate, ingredients were meticulously paired and attention was paid to every single detail of each course. Even the sorbet used to cleanse the palate between courses was an experience. It's a dining experience I recommend at least once in life.

Gretchin Rubin says "the years are short but the days are long."[4] When I initially read this, it sounded funny but it's true. The years seem to fly by and everyday is packed with things to do. If 2020 taught us anything, it was to slow down and pay attention; we had no choice but to have a seat and watch life on most days. I used most of this time to write because I've learned the mind is constantly working - either building or destroying. And if I don't guide the work, the mind is on its own and quite often this means destroying something out of boredom. I spent some of this writing time intentionally finding, documenting, generally bearing witness to delight - anywhere and everywhere around me. It was joyous, unexpected and likely one of the most rebellious acts I had personally ever done. Here's why... For someone who feels

---

4 Rubin, G. C. (2011). *The happiness project, or, Why I spent a year trying to sing in the morning, clean my closets, fight right, read Aristotle, and generally have more fun.* Toronto: HarperCollins.

compelled to always do something, the exercise of just being, just bearing witness to life, required something different from me. Like most of us, I often think if I'm not doing something, it impacts my value at that moment. I learned a great deal about the true value of sitting still and paying attention during the early months of 2020. I was an only child for over 15 years and as any only child knows, you get used to your own company. This time around, alone time felt very different. I found enjoyment in just sitting on a kitchen bench, face poised toward the sun, soaking in each ray in silence. Savoring every flavor the moment had to offer.

Take the time to savor the flavor of your food, savor time, savor the now. And when it comes to food, make sure you're eating good food to begin with because that's always the caveat.

CHAPTER FIVE

Meal Prepping
(Mind Over Matter)

T he walls at my primary school in Kingston, Jamaica were painted with various motivational says, the kind kids need to see everyday. "Education is the key to success. Preparation is the key to life." I remember these very vividly, especially now that I'm older. I'm especially thankful that memory still serves me.

I've found out that some days I'm gung ho about prepping and others I could care less about it. This is a reminder for the days when you could give two craps about prepping... Meal prep! Especially when you're feeling lazy.

Telling you that prepping for the day is imperative is obvious. Instead I'll focus on the importance of developing a daily routine of prepping - it's critical.

It starts with the moment your eyes open. Before facing the day, before checking Facebook or Instagram or email etc., start by centering yourself. The practice of preparing starts as soon as you wake up. Whether meditating, praying, deep breathing, stretching, anything that creates the time and space for you to clear your mind and focus your energy. It's helpful to use this time to set your goals and intentions for the day. It is a habit that must be developed; it doesn't just happen naturally. At least not for me.

The fact is we have the power to change (or not) our daily lives through our thoughts, which connects to feelings and subsequently actions/behavior. There's a whole body of work around behavior and manifestation that explains the whole shi-bang so I won't explore that here. Truthfully, I struggled with this concept for a long time. Being a social worker, an immigrant, someone who's travelled a tiny bit and has experienced and witnessed a small portion of the suffering that exists both locally and globally - it felt disingenuous for me to believe the power to change your actual circumstance lies in our thoughts. It felt too simple, almost insulting. Here's how I resolved it, we're all in different spaces, suffering in different ways based on our circumstances. If you asked Elon Musk what brings him pain and suffering I'm certain he'll have an answer, a different one from myself or another random person but suffering exists no matter who you are. The common thread is how we think about our suffering, whether we think about it at all. And subsequently what actions we take as a result of our thoughts.

The point is the practice of preparing starts with how you think, how you talk to yourself, and what you do throughout the day. This practice extends into cycles of preparing, planning, executing, tracking and adjusting - they are constantly happening around us. We have to be keen on observing these cycles and riding the waves as they come.

I mentioned earlier that I'm not the best cook, but I'm a great helper! My mom will attest. One of the more labor-intensive Jamaican dishes (all the real Caribbean cooks will be laughing in a second) is rice and peas. When made from scratch, and that's the only way traditional Jamaicans will make it, the recipe calls for fresh coconut that's cut into small pieces, then blended with water to get coconut milk. This is only one ingredient! Albeit a critical one because the rice and peas CANNOT live its best life without this. The full dish includes boiling down peas, seasoning the pot with spices and fresh herbs (thyme, scallion, ginger, one whole country pepper) and simmering down the mixture to ensure the milk is fully cooked- otherwise, you risk diarrhea (and nobody wants that). All of this! For rice with peas. But it's worth every step. I've spent many a Sunday morning cutting coconut into dime-size pieces, prepping seasoning and watching the pot. This was one of the first times I realized the importance of preparation in meals. This elaborate dish is only made simple when you prep (often the night before, if you need to "soak the peas") or have an amazing helper prepping for you.

If you've ever had good Black cake (AKA Jamaican Rum cake) you've likely tasted the fruits of sometimes YEARS of preparation. Yes the cake itself is made fresh, but months - some time years - before the sugar and butter gets acquainted and starts getting whipped into shape the fruits need to be soaked in the chosen alcohol concoction. For some this is Red Label wine; for other's it's Port wine or some other mixture but these fruits are married to the concoction. They get to know each other so deeply they become one and the same. So much so that by the time the fruits are added to the freshly made cake batter, they are oozing with alcohol. When tasting the finished product you can tell almost immediately whether the fruits were pre-soaked or not. Preparation at its finest.

There is immense power in developing a routine of preparing your thoughts; it supports being intentional in our actions (small and large). It requires work. And if you have a tendency to procrastinate like me then prep work rarely sounds enticing. In this instance, I focus on the end goal - knowing the end makes the preparation worthwhile.

Stay ready, so you won't have to get ready.

CHAPTER SIX

Simmer Down The Gravy

(Soul Food)

There are foods that feed your spirit and soul; seek those everyday. Treat them like daily devotion. Sometimes they're comfort food, always scrumptious to the taste. Just the mere thought of it and you can sense your mouth watering in the back right corner.. It's typically not fast food, although the fries from Checkers does something special to my spirit. More often, soul food means home-cooked meals made with love and care. By now, you get the point.

In a fast-food world, soul food takes time and attention. It's slow-churned, simmering down to the type of gravy that seamlessly marries all the ingredients. It's the type of food that brings with it fond memories; after you've savored the last bite, you feel full in ways words can't fully describe. The type of food that requires what can only be described as magic, some call it "putting your foot in it." Making it from the recipe just doesn't quite cut it. It requires a level of folk-lore instruction that only certain teachers and cooks can manifest in the kitchen.

Growing up, my mom would always tell me two things - the first was, "Those people (actors and actresses) on T.V already made their money." Now, as a kid, I would roll my eyes and think - she just doesn't want me to have fun. As an adult, I now know this is an absolute fact. It's ironic how right your parents are in hindsight. The second thing she'd say was, "Eat good food." And by good, she meant fresh cooked meals with natural ingredients.

Growing up poor meant trips to fast-food restaurants were rare. But my mom would still find ways to make "Treat days" possible. We'd have Chinese (this was huge in Jamaica when I was a kid) or jerk chicken from the local jerk man on Ben Johnson day[5] or maybe the mall for some Kentucky Fried Chicken (KFC) on occasion. These were occasional trips, because a significant portion of my meals were home-made. I consider my mom to be a chef extraordinaire. This is precisely where my love of food began. She is an ardent believer that freshly cooked meals keep your thinking sharp, especially for growing children. And because of this, she would cook every day, if not every other day. I never quite understood her insistence on always cooking at home until I became older and learned the connection between what we feed our bodies and our overall health.

As a living organism, it's impossible to consistently feed the body trash (processed foods) and expect to be well. Eat-

---

5 Ben Johnson day refers to Friday. Ben Johnson night is every **Thursday** in Jamaica when food is scanty in the house. This is a time when everyone eagerly awaits payday to do the Friday supermarket shopping and the Saturday market shopping. Source: 'ben johnson' night - Jamaicanwww.jamaican-traditions.com › ben-johnson-night

ing fresh/alive foods consistently is what I consider health-care. Now, I'm not down playing illnesses that require medical intervention but I am suggesting that healthcare starts at the dinner table and in the kitchen. As you can likely tell, I eat most things. I'm not vegan (yet) but I'm on a journey that I suspect will one day lead to no meat. I'm not there yet. The point here is we must consistently seek the types of food that nourish our bodies. Food that supports our growth, clear thinking and the development of the living components of which our bodies are made. We must have discernment about what works for us, and this can only come by understanding what our bodies need both generally and those nuances that are unique to you.

It's the same with people, seek people who feed your soul. People who speak life into your situation, not touting rose-colored glasses but positive thinking. People who genuinely believe in life, believe that everything is working for their good. They're typically people who spend time getting to know you well; they tell you the truth without judgment. Well, ok maybe a teensy bit of judgment, cause' you know sometimes we all need additional motivation. I often find these are people who are always learning and consistently recreating new versions of themselves using what they've learned. They are always seeking deeper levels of understanding both within themselves and in their environment. By extension, they support their friends in doing the same.

Soul food, much like soulful ties to others, requires discernment to recognize. Both require an ever-present mind. The former requires active tastebuds; the latter requires building intuitive muscle.

CHAPTER SEVEN

Spit It Out!
(It's Ok To Say No)

S pit it out if it's no good. Quite frankly it's not worth the calories or stress so why bother. The same rules apply to negative thoughts and relationships. We've all maintained friendships/"associationships" whatever we're calling it these days, solely on the strength of knowing that person "forever". Puhleeze **insert eye roll here** let that thang go. It's not worth the stress, aggravation, intense thinking and mental energy. I make it my duty to discard anything I intake that ain't good, be it food, alcohol or d***.

Fun and jokes aside, it's only when we let go of the thing that no longer (or never did) serve us well that we make room for the life-changing thing that can take us to the next level of living our most authentic lives. This is hard; it took a long time for me to accept this truth. And honestly, I'm still working on letting people go some days because my ego won't allow me to accept this perceived failure. My self-talk would be "I should make this work; after all, you should fight for friendships" (or whatever the thing was). The other thing that played a role in me holding on to people and things was my need for instant gratification, this applied more specifically to sexual relationships. I held on to people I had a sexual connection with because I was afraid. Afraid I wouldn't find that connection again, or afraid of how I would look to other people because ..you know..."we're counting bodies" and such. Talk about limiting beliefs!

On one of those milestone life events, graduation I think, I was cake shopping. It was so serious; I was testing cake from bakers to make sure it not only looked amazing but tasted great too. Now, we've all experienced cakes that look great, elaborately decorated, but the fondue is disgusting. Needless to say, after three tastings, I was just about ready to resign to the idea that maybe I'll need to give up good taste for great decor. That was until I met the final baker; she was professional, had all the bells and whistles AND her cake tasted amazing! I was so glad I hadn't settled.

The other instance that comes to mind is dating. Every now and then, I meet someone who looks great on paper. Smart, articulate, well-travelled, ambitious, most of the bells and whistles. After a few dates, you get a sense for a person's vibe, their values, certainly their habits if you're paying attention. Every now and then, the paper guy would make an appearance and I'm tempted to compromise some things because they check off many other "boxes." Lord what a mistake. As you can imagine, the values that I compromised on in the beginning are often the same ones that end up being the demise of a short-lived interaction camouflaged as dating. I had to get to the point where I was ok saying "No," to that person. No matter how many boxes they checked on paper. They may have been great people...just not great for me at that time. I had to calm my anxiety with the following self-talk. The anxious part of me wanted to just make it work. I'd say to myself, you'll learn to love that thing you hate now, maybe you're being too picky... you know all the things we say to ourselves when the current option looks too good to pass up. This self-talk was swiftly followed by the B side, which is - what's meant for you will never miss you. WHEE-WWW LET ME TELL YOU this can be a hard pill to swallow! Especially when what's in front of you seems immensely appealing and at that moment, it feels like there can't possibly be anything better. It takes faith in something greater to say no.

While I'm never 100% free from these thoughts, I am now more conscious and aware of them. Through increased awareness I now more consciously decide the direction things take instead of moving at the whim of my ego or being driven by fear. Whether it's avoiding tasteless calories, negative thoughts or ending toxic relationships, the same thinking applies.

We must let go of relationships and people who look good -but don't manifest love and growth in our lives. It can be that simple. Only then do we make room for people and experiences that support us in nurturing ways.

CHAPTER EIGHT

Brawta
Yes, You
Should Try It!

Yes, we've all heard it before - variety is the spice of life. Pun intended. There's so much value in trying diverse cuisines. You'll learn very quickly that we are more alike than different in the way we cook, the things we eat, spices we use, sauces we sope up with various bread etc. Become a YES woman/man in this arena! Say YES to anything at least once - especially fried scorpions at the market in the middle of Wangfujing Street. (Ok, most things! Boundaries are a real thing.) There are few experiences as exciting or interesting than sharing a meal with someone of a different culture. It's like returning home and hearing about everything you missed.

As a grad student, I ventured to Beijing to study abroad. It was the first time I truly had to practice "just try it" as a mantra. There were so many foods in the Asian cuisine that, until that point, I hadn't tried before; eel, duck, scorpions...just to name a few. Being with an incredibly encouraging group of people created a safe space to try what felt like scary things. During school-related visits, we'd have opportunities to try different foods. One afternoon we had free time to roam Wangfujing Street, and fried scorpion on a stick is a thing there. It took a while for me to get on board. I watched a few others try it, and survived, so I thought - when again will you be here trying scorpions for the first time? So I tried it. And clearly lived to tell you the tale. They taste like anything else that is deep-fried in grease - crunchy. Almost a decade later, I remember little about the student exchange sessions, but I fondly recall every detail of our excursions and the texture of all the new foods I tried—the feeling of apprehension right before that first bite, still fresh in my mind. My classmates encouraged me to just try it.

Much like cuisines, variety is imperative to life and happiness. There's incredible value in trying different hobbies, especially when you may suck at them. One of the most potent examples I can recall is my adventures in skating. As a child growing up in Jamaica, I never learned how to skate. Skating isn't a thing; there are many other things (like Dandy Shandy, Chinese Skip, Hop Scotch and plenty others). As a young person and later in adulthood, I thought skating was fun. Since skating is a thing in the U.S, I would go skating with my friends. The rink would always be crowded, the DJ bumping the best music; perfect for pretending you're in a skating competition. I was looking cute, jeans hugging all the right corners and ready for the skating scene.

I knew nothing about skating much less standing in skates. So, you can imagine the moment the skates attached to my

feet it was like newly released jacks[6] on ice...legs going every which place. After a few minutes of trying to navigate the
crowd and gently making my way to the center while clinging
for dear life to my friend's shoulder. I resigned at the kiddy
practice corner. This is a small square tucked away from the
main rink. Hold your laughter for later; the story gets better.
So there I was in the kiddy corner, thinking to myself- I'm not
giving up. Furthermore I can't just sit here and do nothing.
So I started making my way around the edges, this time holding on to the wall. Then I let go. I tried to stand up straight.
Immediately, I started my descent. All 5' 11" and 150lbs of
me. It's a long way down and the hardwood floor of the rink
is unforgiving. I landed on the back of my head. I remember
immediately thinking, "I'm pretty sure I just buss my head
to the white meat." For years after that incident, I avoided
the rink until my brother became an avid skater. He's talent-
ed, he's also one of those people who excel at whatever they
put their energy to. He's a people person. He inspired me to
try skating again. I signed up for Saturday lessons in January
2020. After the very first lesson, with toddlers who were incredibly patient with me, the pandemic hit and shut down
my already fragile effort to try something new. But I plan to
resume these efforts as soon as it's safe to do so.

Hobbies (whether skating, cooking, playing an instru-
ment etc.) are an extension of yourself. The larger your sense
of self, the less likely you'll feel sad or threatened when one
part of your life isn't going so well. I've proven this in my
own life. When I connected my sense of success and worth to
how well I did in one or two areas of my life (typically work)
the minute something wasn't going well, I felt devastated.
The more I expanded my definition of success, expanded my
sense of self to reflect all the possibilities, to reflect the myr-

---

6 Jacks is one of the oldest and most widespread games in the world. All
jacks games share a strategy: toss a ball in the air and scoop up pieces
before the ball bounces. Source: https://www.toyhalloffame.org/toys/
jacks

iad of things that interest and inspire me (like writing, hiking, travelling, cooking, creating) - the less impact I felt when something didn't go right in one area. It was as if the more I broadened the definition of success to reflect my interests and abilities; a stronger cushion was created to soften any blows that were sure to come.

Gretchin Rubin covers this beautifully in her book *The Happiness Project.*

Nowadays, social media sites (i.e. Living Social, Meetups, Groupon etc.) have made it extremely easy for us to connect with others and explore our interests. I've tried meetups for stand-up comedy, real estate groups, bike riding, running, etc. I didn't always connect with the people I'd meet but I always enjoyed socializing and the comradery. If nothing else, it was a good stress reliever.

As someone who has tried various creative outlets over the years, I can tell you - you lose nothing in trying. Somewhere in my 20s I started a writing space with an old friend. While we're no longer friends, we shared great experiences. We both enjoyed creative self expression and writing was one way to do this. So we created a space where we could write whatever we wanted to, using pseudonyms. I'm not sure why we decided to do this; I surmise we wanted the comfort of anonymity. But we wrote our feelings in that space, never sharing it publicly though it was a public site. We wrote until we didn't. And the space came to a quiet end, without any fanfare. It had served its purpose and we moved on. Years later I would create another writing space[7]; this time solo, this time shared publicly. I still recall those early experiences with sweet emotion. Grateful to have done that work in that time and space.

---

7 This writing can be found at girlletmetellyou.org.

Being open to learning from others, hearing the stories of others, feeling the connection that is perennially true across the human experience is invaluable.

I encourage you to try a bunch of different hobbies, intentionally creating opportunities to spend time with people unlike you. Intentionally expand your sense of self and subsequently your definition of success. It's in uncomfortable spaces of learning and trying something new that you find your niche. You'll find experiences that bring you joy, experiences that you'd quit your job and do for free, you'll find meaningful connections with others that you won't find should you stay confined in your comfort zone.

Deeper Levels Of Yummy

*I*f you find it helpful to expand on the brief lessons shared, included below are a handful of prompts for each chapter to deepen the discussion. Life often rewards curiosity and requires action that pulls us beyond our comfort zone. The following prompts are shared with this intention.

* More Than A Sweet Treat!*

Failing fast and letting go can be difficult. ***Suggestion:*** Think of a goal or plan you've been working on for some time. Have you been sticking to a plan that doesn't appear to be working? *In the midst of a pandemic, there is no shortage of plans gone awry.* Write it down.

What have you learned, so far, about why your original plan didn't work? Considering what you've learned, how can you apply your learning to change course? Now, rewrite your updated plan and get to doing!

Who's coming to dinner ?

The company you keep is critical to the quality of your life. This has nothing to do with class and everything to do with values, character, habits and how your companions express love in the world. *Suggestion:* Consider your life as a dinner party; who are your guests? Who would you think twice about inviting? What would the dinner conversation be about? How do you feel as you host and observe your guests at the party? Who's helping you haul out the trash and scrape the bottom of the rice pot when the party's over?

Commit to the Meal

Commitment is the practice of consistency. One of the most powerful acts we can do for ourselves, and by extension for others, is consistently keeping small (and large) promises that we make to ourselves.

Suggestion: If you don't already have a "signature" meal, spend some time thinking about what this may be this weekend. Something you find delicious, that you would eat every day if you could. It may come from fond memories with family (maybe something your grandparents used to make), a childhood (or adulthood) favorite, or maybe from your travels.

If you already have a signature dish, consider teaching someone else how to make it- or make it for someone! Maybe for your partner, a girls night cooking class or sharing the recipe with someone you adore. Have fun with it!

And if you're a professional chef and beyond sharing your signature meal - think about a long-term goal you've been working on. Consider what you can do today to move you closer to that goal. For example: If losing weight is your goal. Today's small action may be deciding to write down everything you've eaten. (Whether it's writing down what you ate, trying a new workout, or deciding against the creamy extra dressing etc.) The hack for this one is being consistent in small ways allows us to practice consistency - the same skill is needed for large goals.

Finally, the secret to great oxtail

The paradox of time is all there ever is - is right now - yet in this moment lies both history and the seeds of the future. The practice of living is primarily about existing in the current moment- being conscious. We can only truly savor what we are consciously aware of. **Suggestion:** How do you practice being in the moment? How do you manage a roaming mind and racing thoughts? If you don't already have a mindfulness practice, try this: Find a quiet place (yes, a closet will do), have a seat comfortably (don't be too concerned about sitting with your legs crossed, it's more important that you feel comfortable), take a few deep breaths, then close your eyes. Focus your attention on breathing deeply for 1-2 minutes (feel free to set your phone's timer using a gentle alarm). Tune into the rise of your stomach and chest on the inhale, and let everything go when you exhale. Start slow, with a short amount of time. Be patient with yourself. Be ok with the process feeling imperfect. It's a practice that only gets better the more time you spend actually doing it. Try it this weekend. Heck, try it right now!

If a quiet mind feels impossible to get to, start by jotting down all your roaming thoughts. All the ideas that are ruminating and running through your mind. Shifting roaming thoughts from mind to paper often leaves a bit of mental space for quiet.

Meal Prepping

Everything starts in the mind and preparation is no different. **Suggestion:** Consider self-talk. What do you say most often to yourself? One way to slow down and capture this is to keep note of your day. I don't suggest using your phone because if you're anything like me, the moment I get on the phone for one thing - I'm off on a tangent doing everything else and down the online rabbit hole. Get a good pen and paper, keep it by your bedside. Have a separate pen and paper that you keep with you throughout the day. When you wake up, write down what you're thinking. What are you telling yourself about your day? Take another pulse at lunch. Then again at dinner. Try this for a few days, maybe a week. See what you find. When you have a sense of what your thoughts are, you can better move forward with deciding what, if anything, to do about them.

Simmer down the gravy

You are what you eat. And if you believe that, and value yourself, then quality food matters to you. To be clear, I'm not pretending that access to quality food is easy. That would be hypocritical and is worthy of a separate discussion that extends beyond the reach of this short body of work. What I'm highlighting here is the importance of intentionally making the connection between what we eat and our bodies. *Suggestion:* Consider the foods you primarily eat (maybe 5 out of 7 days of the week). Are they primarily fresh (vegetables, fruits etc.) or processed (packaged with chemical preservatives)? How do you typically feel after having a meal? If you were ill, are these foods you consider nourishing?

Spit it out!

Being confident in saying no is about the importance of boundaries. We betray our own boundaries for various reasons and often, it stems from what we believe we deserve (and visa-versa, sometimes we don't believe we're worthy of great things). *Suggestion:* Think of a negative thing you say about yourself. There's typically a lengthy list since it can feel easier to consider negative thoughts. Write it down. Now, read it. Then, examine and challenge this thought. Is it factual? What evidence do you have that it's valid? Identify a positive *replacement* for this thought. Write it down. Put it in a place that is visible to you every day (maybe the bathroom mirror). Say it out loud to yourself. Repeat it to yourself throughout the day over and over, and over, and over, and over....you get the idea.

Yes, you should try it!

Expanding our sense of self and building self-esteem requires that we create opportunities to learn and practice new things. **Suggestion:** This week, check out a "Meetup" group online, or maybe your community message board for groups in your area about something you're interested in doing. If you already have a hobby that you practice but haven't done so in a while, schedule time to do so in the coming week. Maybe you enjoy skiing, schedule a weekend with friends for the winter season. Or maybe you enjoy cooking, check out a free online cooking class often sponsored by libraries and other groups. Check out the bulletin board of your local library or community center; they typically have free or low-cost social and recreational events.

Bu-Nu-Nu-Nus[8]

I couldn't possibly wrap this book without a list of yummy places you should try. It just wouldn't sit right, so if you enjoy great food - this ones for you! Depending on where you are in the world, heck you may even travel solely to try some of these- for the record, they are worth every bit of the travel effort. These are in no particular order, so feel free to hop around the list! Here goes:

1. ***Shrimp and Grits*** from Vonda's Kitchen - Newark, NJ. I'm not typically a breakfast person, with 2 exceptions - one of which is Vonda's for shrimp and grits. The other is when I'm home in Jamaica; during which time I'm not missing a single meal. Back to Vonda's..The consistent flavor of this dish is just marvelous. It feels like home. They pair the dish with warm, lofty Texas toast. I'll tell you outright - this bread is melt-in-your mouth good. Vonda, the owner, is an amazing host who is often checking in with patrons with a warm smile. This place is a must-try.

---

8 Jamaican patois saying used to denote someone truly close to you.

2. ***Curry shrimp and roti (or really anything on the menu that involves gravy)*** from Luukmaan Restaurant - Zanzibar, TZ. I'm a fan of anything in gravy but the curry shrimp here, with flat-bread (aka roti) is heaven-sent. During a solo trip to Stone Town, I had lunch at Luukmaan. In the midst of this bustling space, I felt as though I was sharing communion with the divine while watching cats lounge around on tent tops. It's an experience like no other, and I'm talking about the food, the people, the smiles of passersby....all of it! I returned for dinner and had the fish; it was amazing too.

3. ***Steamed bammy*** from most any Hellshire Beachside restaurant- Saint Catherine, Jamaica. I could go on for days about all the food you should try when visiting my home. But in the interest of poignancy - steam bammy is an absolute must-have (though everything has the potential to make you feel connected to a higher power). Bammy, made from cassava and hardened with a mix of dough, is steamed down in a soup-like broth with vegetables, local spices and seasonings (scallions, pumpkin, okra etc.) MY GOODNESS! I don't think I do this enough justice. Just know the most authentic version of this is on the local beaches (for example Hellshire in Saint Catherine); finding this on tourist beaches is unlikely. It's a meal to itself, since the bammy expands in the gravy making for a thick and yummy consistency. While you're there, be sure to get fried fish on the side. Fish and Bammy go together like peas in a pod, peanut butter and jelly, curry and roti...I think you get the point. My sister Meisha put me on to this dish during a beach day at Hellshire over 10 years ago- my life hasn't been the same since. Put this on your list of must-haves.

4. ***Crepe and Nutella*** from any food cart - probably in any arrondissement - Paris, France. For about 2 euros it's a deliciously wrapped treat. It's served hot; the Nutella is warm and moving slowly enough down the shaft of the crepe that you can catch it before it hits your fingers. My word! While on a trip with friends, this was a staple at every outing and always a win. Especially since there are food carts everywhere, you're walking EVERYWHERE and it's a mobile meal. It all aligns well.

5. ***Roasted fish and banku*** from any restaurant - Volta Region, Ghana. Ok, scene: river-side, lush greenery for as far you can see, sailing downstream on a reasonably sized boat, cool breeze floating past your face and you're slightly concerned about the mosquito situation as night falls. The fish here was so "meaty" I can't even describe it. And I appreciate all that is gravy so you must understand how good this was for me to exit the comfort zone that is juice intended for sopping with bread. This fish is served freshly roasted, so no gravy involved. Let's talk a second about banku, it's gummy texture blends perfectly with this meaty fish. Banku (made from corn and cassava) reminds me of doughy grits...it's molded into a ball and firm enough to hold its shape. You must try this when you're in this area.

6. ***Bofrot*** from street vendors - Accra, Ghana. These golf-ball sized treats are similar to donuts but less dessert-y/lightly sweet. You'll find vendors making batches of these in deep pots perched on top of coal stoves at intersections all over Ghana. They are deep-fried and when this hits your mouth, when your teeth sinks into the softness of the fried dough - I hope for your sake you bought at least three because you'll want every last one.

7. ***Brown stew oxtail*** from Ms. Norma's Kitchen - Home. Truth be told there is no Jamaican dish my mother hasn't mastered. She is a chef. Sure I'm biased, but I have references and receipts. In this space, I'll focus on the oxtail, but understand the curry mutton is other worldly and the gungo rice and peas with coconut milk will make you want to stay for a cooking residency at Casa Henry. I've tried many an oxtail - none like Ms. Norma's kitchen. The trouble is most places serve oxtail loaded with fat and swimming in grease. Typically, making the time to trim the fat is really for those who have a passion for cooking; we all know that soul food takes time. True chefs recognize this upfront work makes all the difference in creating great oxtail. Pair oxtails with a side of steamed cabbage, aforementioned gungo rice and peas and a glass of freshly made carrot juice. It's life changing.

Wishing you a lifetime of yummy eats and yummy experiences that keep you full for the journey.

Acknowledgements

T hank you for sharing this space with me. For spending some time here. I'm excited about the connections you may feel and see in this work.

None of this could have happened without the unwavering support of the following people.

Mom, it's your love of food that inspired this book. Thank you for consistently being unapologetic in how you show up in the world. And for sharing your passion with so many. I continue to learn how to live by watching you.

Justin, you are incredible, smart, funny, creative, kind and capable of achieving great things. I want you to always know this. You're a constant reminder to never be afraid to try new things fearlessly.

Grandma, you are the epitome of unwavering. Thank you for always encouraging me to do my best.

To my loving family of friends and sisters - Candiece, Michelle, Erica, Dacia. My RPP[9] sisters Soph, Meisha and Shar

9Relationship Passa Passa Podcast - website: https://rpppodcast.wixsite.com/home

- thank you for being everyday examples of extraordinary living. Thank you for co-creating a nurturing space for us all to grow.

My brothers - Los and Trev, thank you for making me feel loved, always. I love y'all something deep.

To my beta-readers - an extra big thank you. Who do I think I am with beta-readers!? Thanks for not laughing me out the room but instead graciously making time to review this work.

To the amazing extended village who've nurtured, pruned and encouraged me - Mira, Raphael, Nancy and D. You've spurred confidence in my writing and have been suns in more ways than one.

To readers of this work, and my other musings, to anyone who has ever shared an encouraging word, shared my work or shared your time in support of making this possible. I really appreciate you.

I look forward to sharing more adventures with you all, family and friends, both old and new.

Until next time, *walk gud'*

Index

A

Accra, 22, 50

actions/behavior, 29

associationships, 35

B

Beijing, 39

Ben Johnson day, 33

Black Girl Chronicles, 8

Boundaries, 17, 38, 46

Building wealth one house at a time, 13

C

Caribbean cooks, 30

comfort zone, 42–43, 50

commitment, 17, 23, 44

connection, 9, 25–26, 33, 36, 42, 46

consistency, 23, 44–45, 49

D

Dinner en Blanc, 18

E

executing, 29

F

folklore instruction, 33

France, 49

friendships, 8, 35–36

G

Ghana, 22, 50

goal achievement, 23

Great Oxtail, 24–27, 45, 51

H

habits, 23, 36, 44

Headspace, 25

hobbies, 39–40, 42

I

Intentional living, 17–19, 24–26, 30, 42, 46

Intuitive muscle, 34

J

jacks games, 40

Jamaica, 28, 33, 39, 48–49

Jamaican dishes, 30

Jamaican patois, 48

K

Kentucky fried chicken (KFC), 33

Kingston, 28

L

long-term goals, 22

M

Manhattan, 17

Marshmallow Life, 11–12, 14

Masters of Social Work (MSW), 21

meals

AKA Jamaican rum cake, 30

bofrot, 50

brown stew oxtail, 50–51

crepe and nutella, 49–50

curry shrimp and roti, 49

roasted fish and banku, 50

shrimp and grits, 48

steam bammy, 49

meetup group, 47

mindfulness practice, 45

mistakes, 21

N

negative thoughts, 35, 37, 46

Nwigwe Beach, TZ, 16

NYC, 17, 26

P

pandemic, 19, 40, 43

Paris, 49

planning, 17, 29

positive replacement, 47

predominant movement, 25

preparing, 29–30

R

relationships, 8, 17, 23, 35–37

restaurants

Hellshire Beachside restaurant, 49

Luukmaan Restaurant Zanzibar, TZ, 49

Ms. Norma's Kitchen, 50–51

Vonda's Kitchen, 48

Rubin, Gretchin, 26, 41

S

Saint Catherine, 49

Schaub, John, 13

self-talk, 36–37, 45

short-term goals, 22

Signature meal, 21–22, 44

Skillman, Peter, 12n1

Small wins, 22

social media sites, 41

Soul Food, 32, 34, 51

stick-with-it-ness, 20, 22–23

Stone Town, 16, 49

success, 23, 28, 40–42

T

Tavern, Gramercy, 26

The Happiness Project, 26,
    41
tracking, 29

W
Wangfujing street, 38
writing space, 41
Wujec, Tom, 12

Z
Zanzibar, 16, 49

About The Author

KerryAnne Henry writes stuff you should read. She is a karaoke buff, dance enthusiast, writer and food connoisseur. KerryAnne's traveled four continents and survived at least one pandemic (so far...fingers crossed).

She's served children and families as a social worker for 15 years and is a licensed therapist. KerryAnne holds a Bachelor's degree in Environmental Health and a Master's in Social Work from Rutgers University. She is a daughter, sister, grand-daughter and friend passionate about mental health, spirituality and the interconnection of all things. KerryAnne believes it is by practicing stillness we connect with our true selves, increasing our awareness and ability to manifest our intentions in the universe- this almost always involves yummy food.

More information and her musings can be found at girlletmetellyou.org.

Made in the USA
Middletown, DE
02 October 2021